D1737876

SUMMARY
OF
ULTRALEARNING

Master Hard Skills, Outsmart the
Competition, and Accelerate Your Career

BY SCOTT YOUNG

High Speed Reads

Disclaimer: This is a summary and not the original book.
Buy the original here: https://amzn.to/2ZVuJSA

©2019 High Speed Reads

Please be advised that this is an UNOFFICIAL summary and analysis. This summary and analysis is not affiliated, authorized, approved, licensed, or endorsed by the subject book's author or publisher.

No part of this publication shall be reproduced, duplicated or transmitted in any way or by any means, digital or otherwise, including photocopying, scanning, recording and translating or by any information storage or retrieval system, without the written consent of the author.

Product names, logos, brands and other trademarks featured or referred to within this publication are the property of their respective trademark holders. These trademark holders are not affiliated with us and they do not sponsor or endorse our publications.

TABLE OF CONTENTS

CHAPTER 1: CAN YOU GET AN MIT EDUCATION WITHOUT GOING TO MIT?

SUMMARY

I have never attended MIT, but instead went to the University of Manitoba. MIT was something I simply couldn't afford to do. I realized I was taking the wrong major and had to decide if I wanted to go even further into debt in order to get a degree that was more with my interests. That's when I found a free MIT class online. I took it and was pleasantly surprised that it was much more interesting than the classes I had spent so much money on. So I started wondering, could I learn for free the equivalent of a degree?

I found that some of the classes didn't cover the information quite as well as others. I began to piece together an education with what I had available. Then I realized, as long as I could pass the finals, what did it matter how I got the information? I planned on doing all the classes in just one year. It took time to work out a schedule, but I eventually found a groove. I did manage to complete it in just under a year.

Soon I had a friend tell me that I was on the front page of Reddit. Soon I was having job offers for jobs I hadn't been trying to get. There was a huge debate, was my way just as good as the official way?

My friend and I started a new challenge. We called it "The year without English". We would go to 4 countries and spend a year in each. Once there we would totally immerse ourselves in the language, not even speaking English to each other. While we managed in Spain and Brazil, we had to loosen the "No English" rule when we made it to China and Korea. But, by the end of our year we could proudly claim to have learned 4 new languages.

The same quick learning applied when I tried learning to draw. In a short amount of time, since I had immersed myself in the new project, I would become much more proficient. Soon I came across others that were the same way. They may have their own personal rules for learning but each had some similarities. They would work hard to achieve their dreams. Driven to learn in a way that was almost an obsession, and they often didn't care about the paper that said they could do it. Instead choosing to learn for learnings sake.

Recap of chapter 1

1. I started out simply trying to get an MIT education without going to MIT.
2. I realized I had found a new way to learn and tried it with learning a language while immersed in the culture.
3. There are many other ultralearners out there also.

CHAPTER 2: WHY ULTRALEARNING MATTERS

SUMMARY

Ultralearning is a type of strategy and is self led. You need to be choosing what you are learning and why. It doesn't mean that you have to specifically be teaching yourself, just that you have made the choice. Yet it's also a very intense process. It's not easy and it's going to be a taxing process. It may sound hard, and it is. But it's so incredibly rewarding. After all, how many of us dream of learning another language or learning to play an instrument? You can do this with ultralearning.

Jobs are starting to require more from their employees and ultralearning can help with that. College tuitions are becoming far too expensive for many and yet you are expected to know beyond the high school level to get the jobs that are out there now. Some jobs simply require you to have the knowledge and don't worry about a degree.

The key to ultralearning is to not only have a practical reason for wanting to learn, but because you have the passion to learn. When doing it this way, it shows you that there are so many new things you could potentially learn, if you only apply yourself. You must find the time to apply to it. Be it part time, or a few weeks of intense cramming. It really depends on what your schedule looks like and how much time you have that you can apply yourself.

Recap of chapter 2

1. Ultralearning is important because today's workforce is changing.
2. Jobs require added knowledge but don't always require a degree.
3. The important thing is to find the time to apply yourself to ultralearning.
4. Ultralearning is easier when it's something you're passionate about.

CHAPTER 3: HOW TO BECOME AN ULTRALEARNER

SUMMARY

When a friend of mine named Tristan heard I was writing a book about ultralearning, he suggested that he be my guinea pig. After all, everyone I was speaking to had already become an ultralearner. He wanted to go through the process so that I could document it.

First, he had to pick a topic. After some debate, he finally settled on public speaking because it was something that would be useful for him and that he knew he wasn't great at. Soon he was wrapped up with Toastmasters International and entered into the World Championship of Public Speaking. He immersed himself in learning and his coach pushed him hard. Soon, he was moving up in the competition and beating out those with decades more experience.

What he didn't expect from the whole thing was a career change. Because after he landed in the top ten and word got out how quickly he'd managed to learn, others wanted him and his coach to teach them. Eventually, he ended up starting a consulting career for public speakers.

So how do you start? First, you have to learn exactly what you need to learn in order to hone this skill. Research what it is that you're learning and find where you're lacking. Then, find time in your schedule to only work on that specific skill. It's your time to learn and do nothing else. Then you need to begin to learn. Be ruthless with yourself and figure out what your weak point is. Break it into smaller pieces and learn those smaller pieces before moving on. Make sure you've learned it by testing yourself and make sure you get harsh feedback. If you find yourself unable to retain certain information, figure out what's happening. Make sure you are truly learning it and not just temporarily retaining the information. Then, step out of your comfort zone and push yourself to use these skills.

Recap of chapter 3

1. To be an ultralearner, you need to dedicate the time.
2. Be relentless with your mistakes by finding them and working to fix them.
3. Don't hide from harsh criticism.
4. Test yourself to make sure you have retained the information.

CHAPTER 4: PRINCIPLE 1-METALEARNING: FIRST DRAW A MAP

SUMMARY

The important first step is learning how to learn your chosen subject. This is metalearning. You find out the information is structured so that you know how your particular subject works and what you need to master in order to learn it. In this way, you form a map that will give you the process in which to learn your chosen subject.

Also, the more you learn the ultralearning way, the better you seem to get at learning. This is perhaps due to the metalearning you do and the ability to break down your chosen subject into easier to digest bits. The easiest way to do this is by asking yourself three things. "Why?", "What?" and "How?"

So why do you want to learn what you are learning? Is it just because you want to or do you need to for a specific reason. if it's for a specific reason, like for a promotion, make sure you would actually be able to get the promotion with your newfound knowledge. All that work won't do you any good if they require a degree. So be sure you can get what you want after you learn.

Once you know why you want to learn, you need to figure out the what. Figure out how the knowledge is structured for that particular subject. One way to do this is to take a piece of paper and make three columns. One called "Concepts" another "Facts" and the last "Procedures". After that, start thinking of all the things you need to learn. This doesn't have to be all-inclusive. It's just a loose guide to get you started. The concept column is for anything that needs to be understood. Facts are the parts that need to be remembered. Procedures are the things you will need to practice in order to learn. After that, it's good to underline anything that you think will give you trouble. Once you identify these, start to break them down into smaller pieces to make them more manageable.

Your last question is how you're going to learn it all. Will you give yourself benchmarks to reach your goal. How are you going to measure your success?

Recap of chapter 4

1. Your first step is to find what you plan to learn.
2. Next, you should decide why it is that you are learning this skill.
3. Next, choose specifically what you are learning.
4. Lastly, how are you going to decide you've learned it.
5. Do plenty of research so that you know what path you need to take.

CHAPTER 5: PRINCIPLE 2- FOCUS: SHARPEN YOUR KNIFE

<u>SUMMARY</u>

When setting out to start learning, you have to master the ability to not procrastinate. But why do we procrastinate? Usually it's one of two things, either you don't want to do it or there's something else you would rather be doing. So what is the best way to fight procrastination? Actually, it's fairly easy. Be realistic with yourself about the desire to procrastinate. Once you are able to become aware of it, you can start to make steps in order to not procrastinate. Normally, if you just take the time to start working you will find that it's not as bad as you originally thought. Pushing yourself to get through five minutes will often get you working for much longer.

If after a while you can work for the five minutes but find yourself stopping after that, push for longer. Sometimes it might be a certain situation that causes you to want to give up. Instead of allowing that, push yourself to quit only when you have worked through whatever had you stuck. Often afterward you will find yourself able to push ahead.

Distractions can be another issue to learning. Some things allow you to flow through them effortlessly and distractions aren't an issue. But sometimes you may find yourself struggling. Try not to be too hard on yourself. Research suggests that studying longer doesn't mean you will remember more. Plan how long you'll be studying and if you have multiple hours, try to break it up for different subjects. Find what works for your schedule and go with that. Your studying time may not look like anyone else's and that's perfectly fine.

Try to eliminate factors around you that will distract you and realize that sometimes a task you are learning can just be hard to focus on. For some subjects you may find reading about it harder to learn than if you were watching a video. Try different styles if you're having issues focusing. Also, check your emotions. If you're upset or angry about something else, it can make focusing difficult. Acknowledge the feeling you're having and then guide your mind back to the task at hand.

Recap of chapter 5

1. You may need to learn how to learn.
2. The easiest way to beat procrastination is to acknowledge it.
3. Sometimes learning is more effective when you take frequent breaks.
4. Find what works for you and do it.

CHAPTER 6: PRINCIPLE 3- DIRECTNESS: GO STRAIGHT AHEAD

SUMMARY

One of the biggest hurdles to learning something is the unwillingness to jump right in directly. Instead, people seem to almost avoid the very things that will bring them leaps and bounds closer to what it is they are actually hoping to achieve. The easiest way to be direct with your learning is to spend time actually doing the thing you want to learn.

Many try to learn something and then apply it to the real world. Yet it doesn't seem to help nearly as much as being immersed in the situation and working the problem out for yourself. When you are unable to immerse yourself, create a situation. For example, if you want to learn to code, you begin to start building a website. Give yourself a large project that involves all that you learn. Having that big project to work through will give you much more knowledge.

If that won't work for your chosen subject, you can also try immersive learning. this is a lot like when people want to learn a new language so they go to that country and live it.

Learning to fly a plane, for instance, requires a license. For these situations, you can use something like a flight simulator. If you can't afford to go to France, you can still have a face to face conversation with a French person online to practice.

The last way is what I call the overkill approach. This would be like signing up for a test you know is above your level in order to push yourself harder. Signing up for a competition would be another way. Anything that really drives you to try your hardest even if it may seem impossible.

Recap of chapter 6

1. When learning, find a way to directly learn by doing.
2. Every different skill will have a different way to directly learn it.
3. Finding a way to immerse yourself in your new chosen skill is the best way to learn it.

CHAPTER 7- PRINCIPLE 4- DRILL: ATTACK YOUR WEAKEST POINT

SUMMARY

Often when we are trying to learn a skill, there is a point where things tend to bottle neck. Here, in order to learn the next steps adequately, you need to have the rest mastered. If you are learning another language but don't know many words, you could learn grammar and sentence structure all day but still not be able to communicate well. You can't learn to fly if you don't first know how to take off.

With drills you break down whatever it is that's slowing your progress so that it's easier to understand. Rather than focusing on the whole picture, it brings it down so that it's a much more manageable piece for you to learn.

As you're learning, you do your best to learn it directly. As you go along, you will find a point when you are struggling. That is when you break it down as much as needed in order to find the component that is giving you troubles. Then, once you have that under control, move to the next. Find the aspect that would help you the most to learn and do that first. Everything else can come later. The focus should be on improving as quickly as possible.

There are many ways to do this, one of which is slicing. This is like when learning a piece of music and you find yourself struggling with one section, you repeat that section over and over until you master it. The main factor for learning this way is to find a way to repeatedly work on that one part that gives you trouble until it doesn't anymore. Some even choose to try to do something they can't do, just so they can break down what it is they need to learn and what they don't so that they can focus their energy better.

Recap of chapter 7

1. When learning, you will inevitably get stuck on something.
2. When you get stuck, try to break the problem down so that you can find what the issue is.
3. Focusing on the aspect that is keeping you from progressing will help you make the most progress.

CHAPTER 8: PRINCIPLE 5- RETRIEVAL: TEST TO LEARN

SUMMARY

Trying to learn a new skill often requires some sort of studying at some point. After all, you can't just remember everything you read. Studies have shown that when you test yourself on the information you're trying to learn, you do better.

Some students will try to passively read through in order to prepare for a test, but this doesn't usually help as much as simply diving in and testing yourself. When you struggle to retrieve the information you're trying to learn, you retain it better than if it goes much more easily. So passively studying doesn't work nearly as well as struggling through. Of course, if it's entirely too hard it can cause problems all its own. The key is to be familiar without waiting too long to test yourself.

What this means is that if you want to remember something, you have to practice remembering it. It seems simple enough. The key is to make sure you truly understand those things that you need to know long term. If there are aspects you need to learn but don't need to retain, they aren't as important. But you still need to have the knowledge to know what you will need in order to look it up later.

To practice retrieving information, you can use flash cards. They are easy and can be a very effective way to test yourself. Another is free recall. This is where you read a chapter and when done set out to write down everything you just read. This can be extremely difficult but that is also why it can be effective.

Another tactic is to take something you want to remember but rewrite it as though it were a question in a book. You can also create a challenge for yourself to practice later. Also, refrain from looking up the answer if you feel the need. This struggle will help your mind retain the information in the long run.

Recap of chapter 8

1. Struggling while studying is actually a good thing.
2. When you struggle, your mind is more likely to retain the information.
3. Flash cards are a good way to test yourself.
4. Finding creative ways to test your knowledge can help you retain the information longer.

CHAPTER 9: PRINCIPLE 6- FEEDBACK: DON'T DODGE THE PUNCHES

SUMMARY

Getting feedback is incredibly important. But if someone isn't straight forward with you when giving it, then it's not going to be as constructive. If you put yourself in a situation where you can fail, you are going to get much better feedback than when you know you will be treated nicely.

Overly negative or overly positive feedback doesn't help. Neither does any feedback that doesn't give us useful information. We need to take the feedback and look it over but dismiss anything that doesn't seem to fit with what we're trying to achieve.

Feedback can make us uncomfortable and so we often don't search for it. Yet often it's the fear of receiving it rather than the actual feedback itself that can be so scary. Yet when you find people that are willing to give that brutally honest opinion, we can grow so much faster than if we are given it with love and compassion.

There are three types of feedback, outcome, informational and corrective with outcome feedback being the typical kind you will get. Outcome gives you a general idea how you are doing but doesn't really give you an idea on what you're doing wrong or right. Informational feedback tells you what you're doing wrong but doesn't really give much direction on how to fix any problems you're having. Corrective feedback is the best kind to receive because not only are you told what you're doing wrong but also how to fix it. Unfortunately, this can be harder to get because you need a teacher or mentor that is experienced in order to tell you what you need to do.

Recap of chapter 9

1. Getting feedback can be tough but it's a great way to test your progress.
2. Overly positive and overly negative feedback can be equally unhelpful.
3. Try to get feedback from people who can actually give you the advice to improve.

CHAPTER 10: PRINCIPLE 7- RETENTION: DON'T FILL A LEAKY BUCKET

SUMMARY

Sometimes recalling information can be tough. Nobody knows for sure what exactly causes people to forget things, but there seems to be a few contributing factors.

The first theory is simply that our memory decays over time. This seems to make sense since we can remember what happened recently a bit more easily than things that happened years ago. But there are a few flaws with this idea. One is the fact that most of us can recall older memories with clarity and yet can't remember what we had for dinner four nights ago. This seems to be linked to how meaningful the memory is, but it still shows that some of this theory isn't completely true. While it may have a factor, it's not the only thing that causes memory loss.

The next is interference. This is the thought that our memories are something like the hard drive on a computer. There is only so much space and that some older things have to be overwritten to make room for the newer ones. Sometimes this can be helpful, if you are wanting to forget something painful for instance. Yet if you are trying to learn something similar to something else, it can cause conflicts. your brain can accidently overwrite the information you previously had stored. This is like when you already have mastered French and start trying to learn Spanish and yet French words slip out.

The third idea is that we have simply forgotten the cues to draw up the memory. If you don't recall what the cue was in order to pull up the memory, it remains essentially lost to you.

While forgetting is something that everyone does, ultralearners seem to have prepared for it. One way of doing this is to constantly repeat in order to remember. Shorter bursts of studying where you have to recall the information learned the day before is much more beneficial than trying to cram everything all at once. You need to space it out so that your brain can get the most out of learning. As long as you get semi-regular practice, it can greatly help. This is also how you can make sure you continue to remember your skill once you've reached the goal you set for yourself.

Another way to recall things is to do it so much that it ends up becoming second nature. Much like when you are learning to type on a keyboard, you may struggle to remember the location of certain letters at first. But then over time you won't have to even think about the letters as your fingers fly over the keys. This is similar to another in which you over learn. With this, you give yourself extra practice after you feel you've learned something so that it embeds itself further.

You can also use mnemonics. There are many different ways to use them in ultralearning but the concept is simple. Giving yourself something that links what you know to what you want to learn. This is like when learning a new language and memorizing words, you link them to a similar sounding word in your language.

Recap of chapter 10

1. Forgetting things is a fact we all have to live with.
2. Coming up with ways to recall information can help you retain it longer.
3. Doing something often enough that you don't even have to think about it is one way to make sure you remember longer.

CHAPTER 11: PRINCIPLE 8- INTUITION: DIG DEEP BEFORE BUILDING UP

SUMMARY

Having good intuition about a subject can take you a long way. But how can you develop that? It may not seem like something that can be learned, but it most certainly can be.

When a problem gets difficult, you can't just give up. This can mean going farther than others normally would when trying to figure something out. So, if you come across a problem you feel you can't possibly find the solution to, dig out a timer. Set it for ten minutes and tell yourself that you're going to push yourself a little further in those next ten minutes. With luck, you'll push through and find the answer. If you don't, you just ensured that when you do finally find the answer, you will be more likely to remember it.

Another way is by trying to recreate others results. That doesn't mean simply following along. Instead, see what they did and try to figure it out for yourself. Yes, you may have to try many different times, but you will continue to learn until you finally reach the desired result.

Also, make sure you ask a lot of questions. Many don't want to ask questions because they feel it makes them look less knowledgeable but in reality, it helps. You can't trick yourself into thinking you know something that you actually don't.

The key is to keep at it but also make it fun. If you aren't enjoying yourself, it will be much harder to learn. Approaching it as if you are exploring something new will help you learn much more than simply trying to bulldoze through.

Recap of chapter 11

1. To gain intuition about something, you need to really know it.
2. Sometimes asking dumb questions is the best way to make sure you really know something.
3. Following along doesn't do nearly as much for your memory.
4. Trying to recreate something on your own may take a lot of time but you will be more likely to learn it completely.

CHAPTER 12: PRINCIPLE 9-
EXPERIMENTATION: EXPLORE OUTSIDE
YOUR COMFORT ZONE

SUMMARY

Van Gogh learned to paint using this last style. He wasn't able to learn in a more traditional setting so he was largely self-taught. He would find others to copy and do so over and over again. he wouldn't give up and would continue to try to make it work. His own art through the years shifted and changed as he tried new things. He would try many different things and always worked tirelessly. Taking what he needed as he learned to copy different styles, he eventually found what worked for him and continued.

When you are first learning a new skill, you need to follow someone else's example. You'll start by building the same skills as everyone else until you have the basics down. After that, you will begin to start finding your own way of working and doing whatever you are studying. After that, it becomes harder and harder to find others to learn from. That's where your specific skills begin to become more pronounced.

With experimentation, it helps ensure that those skills don't go to waste. In the beginning, you are simply acquiring knowledge. But in order to get better, you have to try different things and solve problems. This causes you to learn and grow by leaps and bounds.

One way to experiment is with the resources you use. Perhaps choose a book or class and use it completely for a certain amount of time. Then, you can take a moment and decide if that method is truly working for you or not.

You should also experiment when it comes to figuring out what you should learn next. If you're learning a language, at some point you may wonder what part you should move to next. Try various things and see if you have the knowledge to learn that next step. If you don't, you have a better idea of what you could study next.

Some of the more artistic things you can study will also bring your own personal style. Once you feel you've learned enough, you can begin to find your own way of doing things. This can help you find what really works for you and what doesn't. As you explore you learn and grow.

In order to experiment you can try a few different tactics. One of which is to copy and then try to create. Or you can compare your methods side by side. This can help you find what works best for you personally. Another is to try something completely different. If you're used to pencil drawing, try painting, for example. Experimenting allows you to push your boundaries and try new things that accelerate your learning.

Recap of chapter 12

1. Experimenting can really help the learning process.
2. When you try different ways of doing things, you're building your knowledge.
3. Even if you find that something doesn't work for you, you're still learning.
4. Trying other people's approaches can help you learn faster than trying to figure it out yourself.

CHAPTER 13: YOUR FIRST ULTRALEARNING PROJECT

SUMMARY

By now you are probably ready to try your hand at ultralearning. But there are a few key concepts you should keep in mind before you begin.

The first step is to do your research. If you want to set yourself up for success, make sure you do plenty of planning. You need to know what topic and the scope you are going to study. Decide on the main resources you plan to use and have an idea what others have done to learn the same thing. Begin to think about how you are going to use that skill in a practical way. Then, create a backup plan for your materials.

Next you'll have to schedule time for yourself. Find little chunks of time rather than trying to cram it all in one sitting. It's also useful to give yourself a deadline to learn by. You may not stick to it strictly but it will help you prepare mentally for what you're planning to do. If it's something that may take a while, give yourself a test week to try out your schedule. Then you can adjust as necessary without feeling overwhelmed.

The next step is to simply start. Make sure you're prepared and are ready to focus. Ensure you're learning in a way that will help you use the skill later and create drills for yourself. Ensure you can remember what you're learning and find a way to get feedback.

When you're done, spend some time looking back on your results. Is there something you would have done differently? Not every project will be a success, so it's important to learn and see what didn't work for you so you can correct it. And don't forget, once you've learned it you need to keep using it to retain that new skill.

There are alternatives to ultralearning that may work better for you for certain subjects. The most important thing is to always be a student and never feel as though you have reached the top.

Recap of chapter 13

1. When you start your project, plan it out to set yourself up for success.
2. Have a plan and give it a test run to make sure it will work for you.
3. When you finish learning or if you give up, make sure you analyze how things went.
4. Have a plan for retaining the information.

CHAPTER 14: AN UNCONVENTIONAL EDUCATION

SUMMARY

Some wonder if we can raise ultralearners. There have been others who have raised children to excel in certain subjects, making them appear to be genius'.

If you're hoping to raise an ultralearner, the important thing is to start early. The education should start no later than the age of three and specialization by the age of six. Younger children learn faster, although we aren't quite sure at what age this begins to change. the child needs a specialization eventually, even if they are taught a broad range of things. Then, when they are practicing you need to make it like play time. As long as it's fun and engaging, the child will learn. Work and play can be the same thing.

Help them set a learning goal that inspires them. They have to feel inspired in order to put in the work required. Let them feel as though they could be good at whatever they are learning. You don't study something because you are already good at it, after all. You study it because you hope to be good. It simply depends on where the aim is. As an ultralearner, the learning itself needs to be a priority. There needs to be a certain amount of time that is focused on that one skill.

Recap of chapter 14

1. It is possible to teach ultralearning at a young age.
2. Children should begin no later than three years old.
3. As children get older, it becomes harder to learn.
4. Specialized skills should be started no later than six years old.

IMPORTANT FACTS RECAP

Recap of chapter 1

1. I started out simply trying to get an MIT education without going to MIT.
2. I realized I had found a new way to learn and tried it with learning a language while immersed in the culture.
3. There are many other ultralearners out there also.

Recap of chapter 2

1. Ultralearning is important because today's workforce is changing.
2. Jobs require added knowledge but don't always require a degree.
3. The important thing is to find the time to apply yourself to ultralearning.
4. Ultralearning is easier when it's something you're passionate about.

Recap of chapter 3

1. To be an ultralearner, you need to dedicate the time.
2. Be relentless with your mistakes by finding them and working to fix them.
3. Don't hide from harsh criticism.
4. Test yourself to make sure you have retained the information.

Recap of chapter 4

1. Your first step is to find what you plan to learn.
2. Next, you should decide why it is that you are learning this skill.
3. Next, choose specifically what you are learning.
4. Lastly, how are you going to decide you've learned it.
5. Do plenty of research so that you know what path you need to take.

Recap of chapter 5

1. You may need to learn how to learn.
2. The easiest way to beat procrastination is to acknowledge it.
3. Sometimes learning is more effective when you take frequent breaks.
4. Find what works for you and do it.

Recap of chapter 6

1. When learning, find a way to directly learn by doing.
2. Every different skill will have a different way to directly learn it.
3. Finding a way to immerse yourself in your new chosen skill is the best way to learn it.

Recap of chapter 7

1. When learning, you will inevitably get stuck on something.
2. When you get stuck, try to break the problem down so that

you can find what the issue is.

3. Focusing on the aspect that is keeping you from progressing will help you make the most progress.

Recap of chapter 8

1. Struggling while studying is actually a good thing.
2. When you struggle, your mind is more likely to retain the information.
3. Flash cards are a good way to test yourself.
4. Finding creative ways to test your knowledge can help you retain the information longer.

Recap of chapter 9

1. Getting feedback can be tough but it's a great way to test your progress.
2. Overly positive and overly negative feedback can be equally unhelpful.
3. Try to get feedback from people who can actually give you the advice to improve.

Recap of chapter 10

1. Forgetting things is a fact we all have to live with.
2. Coming up with ways to recall information can help you retain it longer.
3. Doing something often enough that you don't even have to think about it is one way to make sure you remember longer.

Recap of chapter 11

1. To gain intuition about something, you need to really know it.
2. Sometimes asking dumb questions is the best way to make sure you really know something.
3. Following along doesn't do nearly as much for your memory.
4. Trying to recreate something on your own may take a lot of time but you will be more likely to learn it completely.

Recap of chapter 12

1. Experimenting can really help the learning process.
2. When you try different ways of doing things, you're building your knowledge.
3. Even if you find that something doesn't work for you, you're still learning.
4. Trying other people's approaches can help you learn faster than trying to figure it out yourself.

Recap of chapter 13

1. When you start your project, plan it out to set yourself up for success.
2. Have a plan and give it a test run to make sure it will work for you.
3. When you finish learning or if you give up, make sure you analyze how things went.
4. Have a plan for retaining the information.

Recap of chapter 14

1. It is possible to teach ultralearning at a young age.
2. Children should begin no later than three years old.
3. As children get older, it becomes harder to learn.
4. Specialized skills should be started no later than six years old.

ANALYSIS & ACTION PLAN

Ultralearning essentially teaches you to learn a new skill in the fastest way possible. Much like people who learn a language by spending time in that country, ultralearning is all about immersing yourself as much as possible into whatever skill you're looking to learn. Yet the way we learned in school may not be the most effective way to learn.

In this book, there are many ways that your traditional ideas on learning will be challenged. It's important to note the author recognizes that we all learn in vastly different ways and he encourages you to find things that work for you. Then, he shows you how to push through any blocks you may have so that you can reach a mastery that you may have thought previously unobtainable in such a short amount of time.

It doesn't matter what skill a person would like to learn, if using the tips in Ultralearning, you will be setting yourself up for success. Because even if you don't completely learn whatever skill you set out to learn, it will teach you much more about yourself and the way you approach every day problems. Developing the tenacity to work through any rough patches will reap rewards in your entire life.

DISCUSSION QUESTIONS TO GET YOU THINKING

1. Have you ever struggled to learn something?

2. Have you ever had a skill that seemed to come to you effortlessly?

3. How do you feel about people who learn at a college level but don't obtain a degree?

4. Have you ever tried to learn a foreign language? What was your result?

5. Do you find you procrastinate even when you want to learn something?

6. Have you ever taught yourself to do something? What was it?

7. How well do you take feedback given to you?

8. Have you ever learned to do something and then experimented with your own way of doing it?

9. Will you be trying the ultralearning approach?

10. Do you think it's okay to start teaching children before the age of three?

ABOUT HIGH SPEED READS

Here at High Speed Reads our goal is to save you time by providing the best summaries possible. We stand out from our competitors by not only including all of the pertinent facts from the subject book but also a personal analysis of the book with action plan included, easy to follow summaries of each chapter including a list of chapter highlights and even discussion questions to get you thinking.

As you can see we go above and beyond to make your purchase a pleasant one. If you learned something beneficial from this book please leave a positive review so others can benefit as well. Lastly if you haven't yet make sure you purchase the subject book, Ultralearning, by visiting https://amzn.to/2ZVuJSA .

Made in the USA
San Bernardino,
CA

56619926R00024